T0098550

THE **3K** MOVEMENT

THE
3K
MOVEMENT
Conquering the Hurdles of Life

CHIDEHA WARNER

NEW YORK

LONDON • NASHVILLE • MELBOURNE • VANCOUVER

THE 3K MOVEMENT
Conquering the Hurdles of Life

© 2020 CHIDEHA WARNER

All rights reserved. No portion of this book may be reproduced, stored in a retrieval system, or transmitted in any form or by any means—electronic, mechanical, photocopy, recording, scanning, or other—except for brief quotations in critical reviews or articles, without the prior written permission of the publisher.

Published in New York, New York, by Morgan James Publishing. Morgan James is a trademark of Morgan James, LLC. www.MorganJamesPublishing.com

ISBN 978-1-64279-673-5 paperback
ISBN 978-1-64279-674-2 eBook
Library of Congress Control Number: 2019907436

Cover Design by:
Rachel Lopez
www.r2cdesign.com

Interior Design by:
Bonnie Bushman
The Whole Caboodle Graphic Design

Morgan James is a proud partner of Habitat for Humanity Peninsula and Greater Williamsburg. Partners in building since 2006.

Get involved today! Visit
www.MorganJamesBuilds.com

This book is dedicated to my family, friends and clients. Thank you for continuing to inspire me to raise the bar.

"When all the dust is settled and all the crowds are gone, the things that matter are faith, family and friends."
– Barbara Bush

TABLE OF CONTENTS

FOREWORD
by Lauren Schwarzmann

I met Chideha in 2008. I had just graduated from Johns Hopkins University, where I studied Public Health and Business. I loved school, but my passion was and still is the sport of lacrosse. I was fortunate enough to play lacrosse at Hopkins and decided to try out for the US Women's National Team during my senior season of college. Being a member of the US National Team has been one of my greatest sports achievements. I moved to Cincinnati, Ohio, to coach women's lacrosse at the University of Cincinnati and continue my education in its Public Health master's program.

With my move to Cincinnati, I got the opportunity to train and work with Chideha. He helped me become the best lacrosse player I could be. I was more confident in my abilities on the field because of my physical fitness and a more confident person. He challenged me and pushed me to be the best version of myself each time I entered the gym. I wasn't just another number in the gym or another client on his to-train list; he cared about me as a person, a lacrosse player, and most important, a friend. He is the best trainer I've ever worked with. He treats his business like he treats his family. That's what real leaders do. Chideha is a leader by example and someone I will have in my life forever. I walked into Fitness3K looking for a trainer and walked out with a friend and mentor for life.

INTRODUCTION

Bringing my best to the fitness arena each day in an effort to help others attain optimum physical conditioning and emotional well-being (the two are closely linked) and continuing to grow a successful business are at the core of who I am and what I love. The marketplace is filled with books focused on nutrition or fitness regimens, and while many of them likely bring value in their own way, I'd rather share with you the driving forces behind overcoming challenges big and small and the keys I believe open the door to our success—not just in fitness or business but in life in general.

Trainers are the lifeblood of a personal training studio. They must be knowledgeable, of course, but also strong communicators, which means having the essential ability to listen, to relate to a potential or existing client, and to ask key questions to understand that client's emotional makeup, challenges and goals. Each client is unique, and successful training is not a one-size-fits-all proposition. Sincerity is crucial for a trainer; if we're playing games and putting on masks just to make a few bucks, we're missing the mark. Clients can smell insincerity, and they know when they're being taken for a ride. They're smart, and they'll disappear, never to return, off to another studio and trainer who truly care about committing to their well-being. And you can bet they'll also share word of their poor experience of a suspect trainer with others.

From a business owner's perspective, I've learned the necessity of wearing multiple hats each day. It's all about earning the respect of our clients and employees, whether that means washing the equipment, cleaning the bathroom, and basically doing all of the unglamorous but essential work. It's about being a good leader and listener and finding ways to make our teammates better, instead of seeking opportunities to criticize them or cut them down. Nobody wins with that approach.

Mentorship is vital to sustained success in business and in life. It's important to seek out others who have had success so we can learn from them, and to share with others our own positive experiences. Coming up short, sometimes, is just part of the game. No one has succeeded every time, at every turn, in business or in life. Coming up short can provide valuable lessons for achieving success when facing a similar challenge the next time around, and hearing of others' experiences and sharing our own can be invaluable learning opportunities for everyone.

Chapter 1

MENTORSHIP

"A mentor is someone who sees more talent and ability in you, than you see in yourself, and helps bring it out of you."

–Bob Proctor

When I consider mentorship and those who have filled that role for me along the way, I first think of my parents. They were my first true mentors; they have helped me to believe in myself and develop strength of character. Their influence is rooted in my first name, something that caused me much trouble as a youngster. The kids at school mocked and bullied me because of it. "Chideha" looked and sounded strange to them, and to me. It caused me much anxiety and harmed my self-confidence.

Isiah & Della Warner, Dr. Warner receiving
2016 SEC Professor of the Year Award

Frankly, it was embarrassing to me. I was bitter toward my parents for naming me "Chideha." Why couldn't they have just given me a normal name, I wondered? Why couldn't I have a name that was easier to pronounce and spell or that just sounded right, especially to the other kids? Why couldn't they have named me something cooler, like my older brother's name (he'd been named after my father), or simpler, like Edward, my younger brother's name? In fact, he'd been named after my beloved grandfather, Edward James Blount, who was such an important mentor to me and whom I admired tremendously. Why hadn't my parents named me Edward before my younger brother came along? I was so upset with my name that I told my parents I would seek to have it legally changed when possible, which greatly bothered them.

My dad explained to me how he and my mom had decided on my name. He said that since I was their second child and they'd named their first after him, they were seeking a unique and trendy name. My father had asked a graduate student from Nigeria who was in one of his classes at Texas A & M about possible African names for a boy. It was during the late '70s, and African names had become trendy for African American babies. None of the names the student suggested to my dad caught his interest, but the student's name did. His name was Chideha.

My dad asked the student about the origin of the name, and he explained that it came from the Igbo Tribe in Nigeria and meant "destiny." My dad was stunned, and he and my mom believed the name showed strength and was different in a good way, and that's when they decided it would be my name. As I matured, I recalled that story and began to feel a sense of peace and understanding about my name. I began to accept and embrace it, and now I can't imagine being named anything else. I'm thankful to my parents for it, and I've let them know that. I try to live my life in a way that best represents the honor of my name.

The origin of my destiny was rooted in a challenge before my birth. My mother was in the final trimester of her pregnancy; I wasn't expected for about another month, but apparently, I decided to arrive early. My dad was out of town on business when my mom went into labor. She drove herself to the hospital, nearly a half hour away. When I was born, my legs were angled toward each other in an unusual and unstable way. Doctors confirmed that I suffered from a severe calcium deficiency and said it was possible I might never walk properly. They put casts on my legs to help straighten them and thought I might spend my life in leg braces. I underwent continued treatments to help remedy the calcium deficiency and physical therapy sessions to help straighten my legs while enduring casts, braces and eventually special shoes. When I was four years old, my parents took me to a doctor in Houston, Texas, who suggested removal of the leg braces and special shoes previous doctors had recommended. I began wearing regular shoes instead. During the next

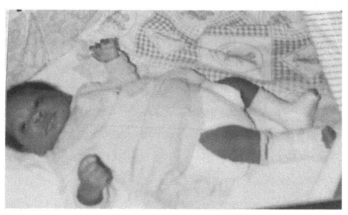

Chideha Warner, 1978

couple of years, my legs began to show proper formation, and I gained strength. I was able to walk and run normally, and in elementary school I joined the baseball team. I was off and running and continued to play sports all through high school. That experience proved to me that it only takes one person to show faith in us to inspire us to take control of our own destiny.

Each of us is a product of our environment in terms of the influence we receive from those we spend the most time with, especially family. That certainly applies to my relationship with my brothers, because the influence they had on me while I was growing up and continue to have on me is considerable. Isiah Jr. is nine years older than I am; he provided a strong, positive example to me when I was young, particularly when it came to physical conditioning. He approached strength training seriously, and his consistent, rigorous workout regimen made a big impression on me. His chiseled physique reflected his efforts. That no-excuses approach stuck with me and doubtlessly provided some of the earliest fuel for my fitness-trainer fire. I'm three years older than my brother Edward, and our closeness in age allowed us to share many experiences and develop a stronger bond. Edward was born with Poland syndrome, a disease that greatly limits the development of chest muscles on one side of the body. At a young age, he was uncomfortable and self-conscious about it, especially around his teammates in the locker room. But Edward refused to be limited by his affliction. He gradually came to accept it and said it was a part of what made him unique.

Isiah Jr., Chideha and Edward Warner

Edward became a strong athlete and student and accepted a track and field scholarship to the University of Maryland, Baltimore County. He received the prestigious Arthur Ashe Courage and Humanitarian Award, an academic and sports-based award reflective of Ashe's strength through adversity and commitment to fighting for one's beliefs, no matter the cost. Edward was known for his high jump prowess and he is among the top two or three high jumpers in UMBC history. He attended law school at American University and is now an attorney in Baton Rouge.

Edward Warner, University of Maryland, Baltimore County

My parents instilled in me a strong work ethic and an understanding that we have to work hard for everything we want and that nothing worthwhile is just given to us. They helped me understand the value of money and to know that I couldn't just toss it around. If I wanted that expensive pair of Air Jordan shoes, for example—and believe me, I did— then I had to show my commitment by saving my money to buy them. Sometimes, learning this lesson didn't go exactly the way I planned it to go. I decided I needed a pair of those $100 Air Jordan shoes when Michael Jordan was bigger than life; he had just won several accolades and was at the top of his game. Everyone wanted a pair of Air Jordan shoes, including me, but I didn't have the money to buy them. As the beginning of school was approaching, my anxiousness about getting those shoes was unbearable. I went to my dad and told him I needed a new pair of shoes, and he happily took me to the shoe store. I shared my excitement with him and let him know I knew the exact pair I wanted. I just knew in my mind that if I got my dad into the store, he would not deny me what I wanted. When we arrived at the store, upon showing him the $100 pair of shoes, his demeanor changed immediately. At first, I thought this was just an initial reaction and that he would understand how important these shoes were to me. I just knew he'd give in. He asked me if I had that kind of money and I replied "no." He then let me know that if I wanted extravagancies like these shoes, I'd have to earn them. He stated that he definitely wasn't going to be paying that price for my shoes unless I paid half. He knew I didn't have the money at that time and stood his ground. I was so embarrassed that I didn't get the shoes and that I expected my dad to cave. That's how my parents raised me; they wanted to make sure I understood at an early age the importance of a work ethic and discipline and how those things were earned.

My dad, Isiah Manuel Warner, grew up in the blink-and-you'll-miss-it town of Bunkie in rural Southeast Louisiana. He learned early in life that he would have to work extra hard to rise beyond the hardscrabble existence many endured in that part of the country at the time. His father, Humphrey,

Erma St. Romain

Warner home in Bunkie, Louisiana

Humphrey Warner Jr. and young Chideha

was a longshoreman and his mom, Erma, was a cook. Neither had more than an elementary school education. But both knew the importance of a work ethic and doing the right thing to overcome the challenges of life in the rural South, and they passed on that knowledge to my dad. The family didn't have much in terms of money or possessions, but they carried a valuable understanding of character and principles. That understanding stuck with my dad, who picked cotton alongside his brother, Charles, in the blazing Louisiana heat to earn a dollar a day to help pay for school clothes. The humidity was so intense that steam rose from their backs as they worked.

When they finished in the fields, they'd walk to town to eat at the restaurant where their mom worked. Segregation dictated that they ate outside, behind the restaurant, in the heat. My dad and uncle claim that when recalling those days, they can still feel the sting of sweat dripping into the cuts on their hands from the cotton burrs. Their work in the cotton fields provided a raw up-close look at the limited opportunity afforded by a lack of education and was instrumental in driving them to seek education and self-betterment.

Charles and Isiah Warner

That awareness, along with his work ethic and belief in what was possible for him in life, fueled my father's push to become a college graduate with a degree in chemistry. He earned a PhD and rose to become vice president of strategic initiatives and achieve Boyd professor status (the highest professorial distinction bestowed by Louisiana State University) at LSU.

Isiah Warner, Southern University chemistry lab 1964

My mom, Della, always had a great knack for keeping me on track in life, for helping me to understand as a youngster that making the right decisions and treating people the right way were essential to building strong character. She let me know that taking shortcuts or trying to get what I wanted at the expense of others was the wrong way to go and would

Isiah and Della Warner, college days

keep me from realizing my destiny. She's always had a keen feel for how business works and has been a great influence on me with my own business decisions. Her parents were college graduates, so, along with her understanding of the core values in life, she knew the value of higher education. Her mother, Eris Blount, and father, Edward James Blount, believed that using that education to help others was essential in trying to make the world a better place. Eris Blount had the special ability to help me realize I was capable of giving more in life, and to see things from a perspective broader than only what was happening with me. And my awareness of the bigger picture increased when she was diagnosed with lung cancer. Watching her battle the awful disease while I was a teenager allowed me to witness courage up close, and it affected me in a big way. As her health quickly and steadily declined, she could no longer care for herself, so she came to live with our family. She was fiercely proud and strong-spirited, and her sudden, forced dependence on others was difficult for her to accept. While the reality of her illness was a serious blow to our family, I accepted it and understood that it was important for me to do my part to help her in any way possible. When I got home from football practice each day, I'd change her bedsheets or help her walk to the bathroom because she had grown too weak to walk unassisted.

Sometimes, we'd enjoy valuable conversations about life. She knew I loved to listen, so she'd share her advice and perspectives with me, and at other times, we'd just sit together in silence, appreciating the love and peace of the moment. No matter how sick she felt, she never complained. She always spoke of the good things in life. Those moments with her during her illness taught me what it means to be truly compassionate toward others. I also learned the value of patience, of what it means to slow down in our busy lives and to stop focusing on ourselves and channel that physical or emotional energy toward someone who really needs it. Those experiences with my grandmother and the inspiration I drew from her led me to commit to volunteering each week at a local nursing home, helping the residents with chair exercises to increase their mobility and circulation. The interaction and shared spirit with the residents through the years has been very special to me. My work at the nursing home is an extension of the influence of my dear grandmother.

Eris Blount, 1963

My grandfather's burning desire for education led him to attain a master's degree from Texas Southern University in the '50s, an achievement nearly unheard of for blacks in that era. He went on to help charter Waverly High School in Winnsboro, Louisiana, and he taught history there. He became principal and coached the girls' basketball team, leading them to three state championships and a runner-up finish. My mom was a player on one of his teams, and his leadership and influence inspired her to become a referee and a coach. Leading by example and staying true to his discipline, he did push-ups and sit-ups each morning and participated in daily runs across campus with his players to improve their conditioning. Sports were a big part of my grandfather's life and he was a stellar athlete. While attending college at Southern University (where my parents later met as students), my grandfather played and lettered in five sports, including football, baseball, basketball, track, and tennis. He saw sports as a strong vehicle for leadership. My grandfather was fearless in always seeking opportunities to improve the lives of others. He never sat back and complained or wondered why things weren't getting done; he just did something about it. Where no path seemed to exist, he simply created it. He focused on what was possible, did his homework, and executed his plan to accomplish the mission. His faith was strong, and failure didn't concern him; he just knew he'd find the way.

He insisted that education was paramount and people of all backgrounds deserved the right to learn. That belief drove him to spearhead the integration of schools in Louisiana and for equal voting rights for blacks. His tireless efforts to help improve the lives of others, especially minorities, created a stir and drew unwelcome and dangerous attention from groups that focused on hate and oppression.

One day, my grandfather returned home from fishing, his favorite hobby, and went to bathe. There was a knock at the door, and my mother, a teenager at the time, answered it. Several Ku Klux Klansmen burst into the house, white hoods covering their faces to mask their identities. They were armed with guns and baseball bats, and they began smashing through the house, screaming for my grandfather. Terrified, my mom told them he wasn't at home, and they slowly began to leave, telling her they'd kill her if she were lying. Just as they were leaving, my grandfather came into the room, having heard the commotion from the bathroom but unsure of the source. The Klansmen grabbed him, pushed him to the floor, and began punching and kicking him and then pummeling him with the bats as he lay there naked. They repeatedly screamed *nigger* at him, my mom, and my Uncle Butch, also a teenager at the time, and held guns to their heads. One of the Klansmen smashed Butch in the face with a baseball bat as he tried to intervene. The cowardly men behind the white masks told my grandfather that word was out about the civil rights work he was doing and that if he knew what was good for him and his family, he'd get out of town immediately. My grandfather was unafraid for himself but was unwilling to risk the lives of his family, so he moved them to Dequincy, Louisiana, where he continued his work in education and pushing for civil rights. He also coached the high school football team there and led them to a state championship. Though the brutal reality of my grandfather's experience is still painful for my mom and me to think about, I believe his story represents the strength and perseverance at the heart of my family and helps others to understand the formidable obstacles he and others had to overcome in the name of progress.

"There is no greater agony than bearing an untold story inside you."

—Maya Angelou

Edward J. Blount

My grandfather died at the age of fifty-three, leaving behind a powerful visionary legacy of work in education and civil rights. His efforts to overcome and achieve, no matter the challenges, have left an indelible mark on me, even decades later. His push to serve others and help them improve their lives inspires me daily and drives me to seek ways in which I may serve.

I am grateful for the positive example my grandparents set daily for my mom and dad and for the way my parents passed on those lessons to me as a youngster and still continue to teach me. The lessons of work ethic, humility, and sacrifice that they taught me, together and each in their own unique way, are a guiding light to me. They will always be my "pioneer mentors," the first ones to help me understand that life is about using our skills and abilities, whatever they may be, in the best way possible as a positive influence on others.

Several years ago, I met a special man named Joe Bitzer. Joe served in the army, where he learned what discipline is all about. Joe was a blue-collar guy and spent some time as a truck driver after the military; his work ethic was ironclad. He later worked in construction, learning the business quickly and climbing the ladder of success. Eventually, Joe became a partner in a construction company, and his vision and leadership skills helped the company to thrive. When his partner wanted to sell his share of the company, Joe knew the opportunity to buy that share was too good to pass up, even if it meant taking a financial risk. He tapped a limited savings account, knowing the money was there to provide an emergency nest egg for his family. Joe's wife pledged her support for the move, and Joe bought full ownership of the company. He made the gamble pay off and never looked back. Joe built Deerfield Construction into a strong, profitable company.

His story spurred my belief that perhaps I could own a business too. Joe helped me realize that with confidence in yourself and a strong vision, anything is possible. He provided invaluable guidance to me, and he still does. In fact, our businesses are located in the same office park, built on land Joe bought as his company grew. Joe trains with me regularly, and his determination and work ethic are on full display in the gym too. Joe is always working hard to better himself, by setting goals and pushing to reach them. He knows that trying to keep himself in good physical condition is an important part of his business and life. His company is a family affair, which is a great source of pride to Joe. He has stepped away from Deerfield Construction and passed on ownership to his sons, Steve and Scott, who continue to grow the company at an incredible rate. The leadership Steve and Scott display daily in running Deerfield has had a major positive impact on me. It's not easy to guide a family-owned company successfully into a second generation. In fact, according to the experts, more than two thirds of family-owned businesses never make it that far. But Joe's sons have made the most, and then some, of their opportunity to lead the company. They continue to build upon Joe's original vision for Deerfield. The company has grown from $7 million in sales in the early 1990s to more than $50 million today.

Joe Bitzer

Opening my business, Fitness3K, in the location shared with Deerfield Construction afforded me an opportunity to meet a man who would in a special way contribute to the foundation of my company. Fred Davis was a longtime building-maintenance man at Deerfield. Like me, Fred hailed from the South and that common ground allowed us to connect instantly.

Fred was nearly eighty years old when I met him and perhaps the hardest worker I have ever seen. He was also incredibly humble. That combination of hard work and humility made a lasting impression on me. Fred seemed to take a special interest in me from the time we met, and we spent a lot of time together. He was one of those guys who had a knack for telling great stories, and we shared many laughs. When I'd ask him if he wanted to train with me in the gym, for example, he'd smile and tell me mowing the lawn and taking out the garbage was all the exercise he needed. He had grown up in Alabama, so he enjoyed needling me whenever his beloved Crimson Tide football team beat my LSU Tigers. But I also savored any opportunity to learn from Fred's life experiences and wisdom. In my gym, the walls are covered with an assortment of framed sports memorabilia and motivational quotes that inspire me and hold a special place in my heart.

Fred organized and hung all of the memorabilia and working alongside him during the process was a joy to me. Mostly, he worked, and I just tried to stay out of his way. When I'd pick up a hammer, he'd tell me to give it to him before I hurt myself. Fred's humility and kindness are part of the fabric of Fitness3K. He was there to help lay the foundation. Fred died a few years ago, but his presence is still there in those frames on the walls of my gym, reminding me daily of his hard work and selflessness and making me want to help others just like Fred helped me. Fred was the furthest thing from a big corporate CEO type, but he was one of the richest men I've ever known in terms of character.

Each of these mentors has played a unique role in helping me along my way in life. From their experiences picking cotton, to obtaining PhDs, performing blue-collar labor to building successful companies, and all points in between, they have helped me to understand valuable life

Fred Davis

lessons. Though each one of them traveled a different life or professional path, the lessons they have taught me share a common theme: sweat, sacrifice, and seeking opportunities to help others get better and push for the greatness inside of them. They've taught me that focusing on only myself is an empty way to live, that the lasting rewards in life come from service to others. They've taught me about the importance of staying true to my belief in what is possible for me in life, which sometimes means taking risks to overcome the odds that may be stacked against me. It also means learning from the mistakes I make so that I don't repeat those mistakes and cause myself unnecessary difficulty. They've taught me about the importance of realizing that no one knows it all and the value I can draw from the advice and experiences of those who believe in me and have been down the path before me.

Mentorship is a vital part of our working together to make our world a better place. It allows us to share the ride in life and learn from others' important lessons that may help improve our own chances of success, while passing on our insight to others to help them succeed in turn. Mentorship means maximizing our belief in the potential of others and constantly pushing them to pull the most from themselves. It means helping them to raise the bar in terms of the success that is possible for them in life. It means being there to support them when they fall, by helping them to get back up and keep grinding. That rock-solid support is what my mentors have provided to me during my journey, and it means everything to me to try to do the same for my clients.

3K Movement Action Item

As someone who had several obstacles and pitfalls along the way in the beginning of their career, I know firsthand what it means to need proper guidance from someone you highly respect or admire. That's why I want to do my part in giving back to people who haven't had the break they needed or the same opportunities I've had to succeed. Think about whom the mentors have been in your life; what have you learned from them? What setbacks has a mentor shared with you that you have learned from the most? At Fitness3K, we not only want to provide stellar service to our personal training clients, we also want to be a resource for up-and-coming trainers and business owners through our website, our social media podcast, or simply a phone call.

I firmly believe that teamwork makes dreams a reality. Henry Ford once said, "Coming together is the beginning, keeping together is progress, working together is success." I believe in my heart that everyone ultimately wants to be successful in his or her career path but there are times when getting connected or finding the right network is the first challenge. To better keep yourself going in the right direction on your path, visit our website Fitness3K.com to check out the resources available to you or to set up a consultation to explore your journey's compass.

Chapter 2

THE RACE OR THE FUTURE?

When it comes to the name of my company, folks have wondered if whether it is perhaps a nod to some sort of running event, such as the 5K or 3K. Actually, "3K" has a dual meaning to me. One is forward thinking/next millennium, and the other is mind, body, and soul, the three elements of which we are comprised.

I'm a big believer in positive energy and in showing kindness and openness toward others whenever possible. Part of this belief, no doubt, comes from growing up in the South, and from that Southern hospitality thing that runs in my blood. I've always enjoyed sharing that warmth with people, but they are sometimes taken aback by it, especially in the gym. When I became a trainer, I worked at a studio where I was eventually named to the management team. At first, the team members worked well together, with plenty of enthusiasm and good energy and support for each other. Everybody felt like they were pulling in the same positive direction. Then, an ownership change caused an extreme overhaul in the day-to-day operations of the studio, and not in a good way. The energy around the studio quickly became negative, from the top down. Mistrust, jealousy and bitterness among management team members became the norm, and suddenly I felt like I was alone. The positive relationships and teamwork that had been developed had vaporized and everyone was out for themselves. I felt out of sorts, not sure what to do or where to turn. So, I prayed. A lot. Then something happened that would change my life.

During a particularly busy day at the studio, I headed home for a few moments at lunchtime to catch my breath. Upon arriving at home, my phone rang. An attendant at the studio was calling to let me know that an unhappy customer was there with no trainer available to help him. I quickly headed back to the studio, looking to make things right with the customer and lead him through the workout session he desired. I didn't know it then, but my decision to rush back to the studio to help a customer rather than relax for a moment at home would prove to be a defining moment for me. When

I returned to the studio, I introduced myself to the customer; when I told him my first name, he appeared puzzled, with seemingly no comprehension of what he'd heard. That man was Joe Bitzer.

When I asked Joe about his fitness goals, he indicated he was largely there at the urging of his son, who believed Joe's physical wellness was a crucial part of the continued success of the family company, not to mention Joe's quality of life. As Joe and I spoke, I learned about his discipline in terms of his business regimen and about his military background, which I knew were strong positives for me to build upon in establishing a training program for him. We began by setting small, specific goals and continued to increase them. As Joe reached those goals and began to see physical improvement, he also felt better emotionally. He started to enjoy the workout process.

We began to get to know what made each other tick and talked about our backgrounds and experiences; it was the start of a very special relationship. Though the friendship Joe and I shared continued to strengthen as we trained together, the atmosphere at the studio was getting worse. The team unity that had once existed was nowhere to be found, and morale was low. There was constant grumbling from management and my fellow employees. When a trainer whom I respected decided to leave the studio and start her own business, I saw it as an awakening for me. I began to consider my own options. I had no desire to stay because I felt that there was a better way for me. I started to believe that perhaps I too could start a business.

Joe sensed my restlessness during our conversations and started to plant seeds of support for me. He told me his employees were seeking a trainer for the small fitness center at his company and suggested I might enjoy working with them. At first, I dismissed the idea, still somehow feeling loyal to my current employer and caught up in the emotions about how quickly things had gone downhill after the ownership change. I questioned whether the atmosphere at the studio might improve if I just hung in there a little longer, but as the days wore on, I could clearly see that wouldn't happen. I decided I'd take a look at the fitness facility Joe had spoken of. During the tour, I met his employees and there was an air of strong positivity and enthusiasm among them, which was a welcome change from the turmoil of the studio. He showed me the fitness center space, and although it was small and sparse at the time, I envisioned what it could become with effort and additional equipment. There was also a baseball-batting cage on the property, which could be moved into the fitness center space, adding to my idea of what was possible at the facility.

When the studio managers informed our training staff that they were about to implement a policy to double the membership rates for our clients, including many with whom I had worked for a long time, it was the last straw for me. I voiced my concern about the rate increase to management, which only angered them and increased the divide between us. I cared deeply about our customers and the relationships and trust we had built with them over time; I believed it was unacceptable to suddenly spring a substantial rate increase on them.

I confided in my clients about the impending changes at the studio and my plan to open my own business in the center at Deerfield Construction. I showed my clients the spot at Deerfield and shared my vision with them of what was possible there. Some of them stuck with me; others thought it best to stay their course at the studio because it was already established, and I understood that. But all of them seemed to respect my vision for the new facility, and I appreciated that.

The more I shared my vision for the spot at Deerfield, the more my confidence grew. As my confidence grew, it was clear to me what I needed to do. I told Joe of my plan to open a training center at the facility and offered to train the company employees as part of the deal. At Joe's request, I also shared my plan with his son, Steve. I didn't know Steve well, and the idea of sharing my plan for the facility and seeking his approval caused me much anxiety. But when he came into the studio, I seized the moment and pulled him aside and got right to the matter. He was a bit surprised at my plan to leave the studio because he knew I had a strong roster of clients there, but he was open to the idea. When I told him I'd be happy to train Deerfield employees as part of the deal, he agreed. It's strange how things work out when we commit to pursuing our destiny.

Though I had made the decision to start my own business and laid the groundwork for the deal with Joe and Steve, I had not yet told studio management of my planned exit. As it turned out, that day was right around the corner. After an employee meeting at the studio one morning, the studio owner and manager met with me privately, and the atmosphere in the room was heavy. They asked whether I had informed my clients of the membership rate increase. I confirmed that I had. Then they asked about the feedback from clients, and I couldn't hold back. I told them the word from clients was not good, that they had expressed to me shock and frustration at what they saw as an arbitrary money grab. They felt disrespected and unimportant, which was the complete opposite of everything that was essential to building strong client relationships. I had always believed that integrity and trust were at the core of those relationships. The studio owner asked what I felt about the policy, and I said I agreed with the clients. I saw the new policy as unnecessary and toxic to the client relationships we'd worked so hard to establish.

The owner didn't mince words. He told me that if I believed that, I was fired. Even with all of the bad energy that had permeated the studio since the ownership change, I was stunned. After all, I had been training clients at the studio since long before the ownership change and had generated more client revenue for the studio than any of my fellow trainers. The owner refused to hear any of it, refusing to see reason. He told me it didn't matter and that as a trainer, I was easily replaceable. Then he told me to get the hell out of his office. I was crushed. I couldn't comprehend how none of the pieces vital to doing business the right way, including understanding and honoring the value of employee and customer relationships, mattered to him.

I walked out of the studio, got into my car and started to cry. The emotion that had been brewing inside poured out as I digested what had just happened. The meeting was the ugly culmination of attitude and events at the studio that had been leading to a point of departure for me. I had wanted to leave the studio on my terms and on good terms with the ownership, but the owner had forced my hand in a hostile way and left me with no choice. While I didn't know what the future held for me, I knew I was better off being freed from the studio's dark and depressing workplace environment. I called Steve Bitzer and told him what had happened in the meeting and that I was ready for a new and exciting beginning with the training facility at Deerfield Construction.

Steve welcomed the news and gave me the green light to head for my new space at Deerfield. When I arrived at the facility, I nearly collapsed in my office from emotional exhaustion. The internal turmoil that had been building for so long from the friction at the studio and my anxiety about the future enveloped me. I was sad, relieved, anxious, excited: the gamut of emotions. The realization of this new beginning for me and where it might lead weighed heavily on my heart and mind. Then Joe Bitzer walked into my office.

He sensed my unease and didn't hesitate to tell me that if I were feeling sorry for myself, it would be useless. It was classic, matter-of-fact Joe. As always, he spoke it like he saw it. His words shook me to instant reality and the emotional cobwebs cleared. His candor was exactly what I needed, and I was grateful for it. Given my respect for Joe and his sons and the integrity they exhibited at Deerfield, I was committed to following their lead in terms of doing business in the same strong fashion. Though their company and mine were in differing industries, the rock-solid foundation of sincerity, passion, and professionalism they had long displayed at Deerfield would also be at the core of Fitness3K. Starting a business is a tall task with numerous challenges, and no one does it purely on their own.

Fortunately, I was able to call upon the expertise of Pamela Ebel, whom I had gotten to know from the studio. Pamela produced videos for corporations and I'd appeared in some of her projects. She had a strong background in leadership training and business management and had worked with companies of all sizes, from Fortune 500 corporations to mom-and-pop operations. Pamela understood the importance of a well-structured organization and that ethics was essential to the long-term success of a company. Our skill sets complemented one another, and Pamela and I developed a strong business synergy. Right out of the gate, she worked to set up the structure of Fitness3K, we decided upon the Fitness3K logo and collaborated on the company mission statement:

> *Our mission is to help clients attain their fitness goals through knowledge, accountability, quality service, and making lifestyle changes.*

The mission statement set the tone for what I wanted Fitness3K to represent then and still does now. My ultimate intention is to provide my clients with a strong sense of empowerment by delivering on the tenets of the mission statement. In considering the aesthetic, the "vibe" of the gym, it was important to me to provide an unmistakable feeling of motivation and positive energy for my clients while they trained. I decided to include an assortment of powerful inspirational quotes from champions of all genres, including sports and business titans, such as Muhammad Ali and Vince Lombardi. As I mentioned earlier, my dear friend and mentor, Fred Davis, who influenced my life in so many ways, hung those framed quotes on the walls of the gym for me. Fred, who struggled to pronounce my first name, always referred to me in comical fashion as simply "the picture guy." Fred's selflessness remains part of the fabric of each of those framed quotes and of the gym itself.

I scrolled through the personal client-training list I had built over the years and began calling those clients with whom I had worked the longest, including Mary Bishop. Mary became my first client at the studio a dozen years ago and is still with me. Mary had come to the studio seeking training help to minimize the effects of ailments, including arthritis, and we connected instantly when we met. Mary hoped to gain physical flexibility and additional range of motion so she could continue to play golf and tennis. When I called to share the news with her about my new facility, she didn't hesitate and told me she was committed to continuing what we had started. Just as she had been my first client at the studio, Mary became the first to join me as a client at Fitness3K. Mary has shown tremendous training progress through the years, and though now in her seventies, her ironclad work ethic remains an inspiration to me. Her commitment during that phone call to continue our training relationship became a springboard for the phone calls that followed to the others on my client list.

When I opened Fitness3K for business, a core group of eight clients joined me. Soon, that number grew to more than a dozen, and within a year, I was working with more than fifty clients. I had plenty of work ahead of me, but I was on my way and filled with gratitude. I spent much of my time early in that first year of business designing a plan to schedule training classes and serve my clients in the most efficient way possible. At the studio, I had been the first trainer to introduce the idea of group classes at a time when they were not common. I believed in the valuable support system of group classes. The members could lean on each other for additional motivation, push each other to keep getting better, and hold each other accountable to allow the whole group to prosper, all at an affordable price point. I became the first trainer in the Cincinnati area to offer boxing classes, including a Saturday-morning cardio-boxing class open to all fitness levels. After the cardio-boxing class, I offered an "Abs and Glutes" group class. The response to these group classes was strong. It seemed I had hit on an area of need that many clients sought. The group training classes and personal training became a focus of Fitness3K marketing. As part of my agreement with Steve Bitzer to train Deerfield Construction employees, I established a group class for the

Deerfield Construction Company, Inc. Employees 2008

employees. That led to many of the employees seeking to train with me individually. Fitness3K had come out of the starting gate and was quickly gaining momentum.

Then, I received a phone call from a fellow trainer from the studio. The trainer told me the working atmosphere at the studio had continued to go downhill after I left and she was unhappy and seeking another opportunity. I knew the pain and sadness she was feeling and I wanted to help. I offered her a job at Fitness3K and she became the first trainer to join forces with me. She was grateful for the opportunity and excited about what was possible. She also had established a strong client list at the studio, which provided additional value to Fitness3K. I was thankful for her belief and trust in me and felt blessed to be in a position to offer her a job. I was confident she'd connect in a strong way with the female employees at Deerfield Construction.

Her contribution to the cost of equipment for the gym was a great help to me. Though I was not yet in a financial position to choose all the equipment I desired, there were certain pieces that were necessary for the basic functionality of the gym. My fellow trainer and I decided that cardio equipment was first on the list. We purchased a new multipurpose, dual-cable machine for $8,000. While we considered the option of buying an older machine at a lesser cost, we knew that the endurance of the new machine would pay for itself and then some, especially where the satisfaction of our clients was concerned. We also purchased a handful of other machines, including treadmills and leg-muscle equipment. We had acquired the essential core pieces to serve our customers in the best way possible as a young company finding its operational footing.

While the addition of the equipment to the gym was vital, of course, the free space in the gym shrank when the equipment was installed. I studied the layout of the gym and the facility itself, including a wall on the backside of the facility where the batting cage was located. I wondered whether the cinder block wall might be removed, which would create a doorway connecting the main fitness center to that valuable additional space. I discussed the wall-removal idea with Steve and he was on board with it.

The floor in that space was concrete, which is not ideal for clients dealing with knee concerns, so it would need to be altered for comfort. We looked into the purchase of AstroTurf and were lucky to find some for sale that had been used at the RCA Dome, then home of the NFL's Indianapolis Colts. As a big sports fan, I believed that having that turf as part of our gym was a blessing. One weekend morning, some of my clients were kind enough to join me in rolling out the turf, which, given its extreme weight, became quite a workout for us. The addition of the AstroTurf created a significant positive difference in the appearance of the gym. The turf just seemed to pull all the elements together in an inspirational way and provided a unique feel to the gym.

The trainer I had hired was settling into her job nicely and approached me about the possibility of hiring an additional trainer from the previous studio. Word of our new gym had apparently traveled quickly among those we knew in the industry, friends and competitors alike. I knew the trainer about whom she was speaking; in fact, I had been involved in hiring him at the studio. While we had just gotten the Fitness3K gym off the proverbial ground and the budget was extremely tight, I felt compelled to help as I had done in hiring her; it was part of my nature. I hired the additional trainer, but it was a move I would soon regret.

3K Movement Action Item

When people start a business, it's easy to get focused on the business name, taglines, titles, logos, artwork, and other such things. While those things are uber-cool to plan and lay out, what's more important is the quality of service you guarantee to provide, and that includes surrounding yourself with the right people. The people you work with can make or break the positive energy you want running through your place. What guidelines do you have in place to ensure your company's team is aligned with your vision? Have you ever taken a risk in your career or would you take a risk if the chances of a positive outcome were good?

1. _____
2. _____

3. _____

4. _____

5. _____

Dig deeper:

6. _____

7. _____

Chapter 3

IT'S ALL ABOUT THE PEOPLE

I played over and over in my mind my decision to hire a second trainer; although I wanted to help him and believed his addition to the staff could further accelerate the growth of Fitness3K, something about hiring him just didn't feel right to me and my uneasiness was difficult to pinpoint. I told myself to relax and stop second-guessing the move and looking for problems that didn't exist. Unfortunately, however, my hunch proved correct and those problems were about to rear their ugly heads.

The first trainer I had hired was served with legal papers at our gym; the owner of the studio had filed a lawsuit against her, claiming that her employment with Fitness 3K had violated terms of a non compete agreement she had signed while with the studio. The studio owner was seeking $30,000 in damages from the trainer due to a claimed loss of client business. Then the studio owner also served the trainer I had just hired with legal papers, seeking $15,000 in damages for the same reason. As if things weren't bad enough, the studio owner served me with legal papers too, seeking $100,000 in damages. I was stunned. The studio owner's claims were outrageous and unacceptable. His motives in filing the claims went way beyond money. His actions were a thinly veiled attempt to destroy Fitness3K by causing significant harm to the valuable relationships we had worked to cultivate with our clients fair and square over time. I was determined not to let that happen. We had built those client relationships with incredible effort and integrity, and the clients joined us at Fitness3K because of it. They believed in us and had made their decisions to join us at Fitness3K of their own accord, and I intended to fight for them.

The studio owner had dug deep in misleading contract language to attempt to enforce his claim against us. I was forced to hire an attorney, which was my first exposure to how representation in the legal system worked, which starts and ends with money. The studio owner had those financial resources to tap, and I didn't. I paid $3,000 to an attorney just to begin the conversation about the case and then an additional $300 per hour. I was spending money I didn't have to protect my client relationships and myself. I was frustrated and fearful, and I wondered what I had done and where things were headed. I leveled with our clients, like I'd always done. I told them about the lawsuit and that if the studio owner intended to hold them hostage by enforcing the duration of old contracts, I was willing to train them for free in the meantime.

Though my intention was pure, the pressure from the lawsuit grew heavier on me and the trainers I had hired. Our relationships became strained and began to sour, and I became the focus of their frustration. They blamed me for the lawsuits and for putting them in a precarious spot legally, financially and professionally; they even suggested that perhaps I had hired them solely to spite the studio owner and create a rift. Those suggestions couldn't have been further from the truth, but there was nothing I could say to convince them otherwise. Sadly, our relationships deteriorated to the point of no return. Both trainers agreed to mediate their legal cases, and the studio owner tried his best during the process to get them to indicate that I had intentionally crossed contractual lines when I hired them at Fitness3K. Thankfully, despite our fractured relationships, neither of them did so, and I was grateful to them for their honesty. Both trainers found employment elsewhere. I took some comfort in knowing that I had done my best to provide them with a framework of education and guidance that helped to put them in a position to receive those opportunities.

The studio owner had succeeded in breaking up our Fitness3K team. With his case against me, he went to great lengths and expense to decimate my business, but in the end, he settled for only a few thousand dollars. His willingness to accept the settlement confirmed that his lawsuits were indeed never about the money but rather about attempting to eliminate me, and Fitness 3K, as a worthy competitor in the marketplace. But karma has a way of catching up. The studio owner went broke soon after and was forced to shut down his business. After the toll his vengeance and unnecessary and lengthy legal process had taken on me, I felt reborn and more committed than ever to doing what it would take to establish Fitness3K as a leader in the marketplace.

Preparation is paramount to our success in life, especially where business ownership is concerned. As a business owner, possessing an ability to envision, to anticipate what may be coming down the path, whether favorable or unfavorable, is key to keeping the business on the right track. While I didn't know for certain a lawsuit would happen, it wasn't a complete surprise to me. I suspected that my hiring the second trainer would raise the eyebrows of my competitor and former employer, and I attempted to prepare myself, at least partially, for what eventually happened. With a focus on finding ways to create immediate marketing exposure for the gym, I held an open-house event, aided largely by word-of-mouth promotion from clients and friends, who also assisted with setup. The event proved successful in terms of drawing potential new clients to Fitness3K, including a few of my previous clients with whom I reconnected. True to the power of networking, one of them told me that a former client was in fact working at a company just down the street from Fitness3K. I arranged to meet with that former client and his business partner to discuss their training goals and needs and how Fitness3K might be a strong fit for them. Chris, the former client, expressed interest in visiting the gym. I had trained his son and he knew how I worked and what I represented from a character perspective. I had credibility with him. Things were a bit different, however, with Rob, his business partner. In a lighthearted way, Rob made it clear that he had little interest in training and fitness but that he was open to the idea of visiting the Fitness3K facility. That was good enough for me. The pair came to the gym, and both became clients. Though Rob had resisted workouts previously, he was soon hooked. His mindset about the benefits of fitness and training changed dramatically, and he became committed to doing the work. He was "all in," as they say, and he has been ever since; Rob doesn't miss a session, if possible.

He is a great example of the magical power of our mindsets. No matter what mental and physical tendencies we may have fallen into, often by default, we have the power to completely change. All we need to do is decide, commit, and keep working. I'm not saying it's easy, of course, but we often make it harder than it has to be for ourselves with the false negative mental images we build up in our minds about what commitment requires. It's gratifying to see the great progress Rob has made over the years, having committed to fitness, staying with it, and reaping the physical and emotional rewards that accompany commitment. Rob and his wife, Stacey, have provided great support for me over the years, always being there to offer their appreciation and words of encouragement or guidance; for that, I am grateful.

In 2008, I focused on establishing an Internet presence for Fitness3K. Although it seems strange to consider now, at the time, the idea of a company website was still fresh. Many companies in the marketplace were just beginning to grasp the importance of doing business digitally. To put that timeframe in perspective, Apple had introduced the first iPhone the prior year. From a technological perspective, it's amazing to consider just how far we have come in such a short time. Back then; the fitness industry was largely new to the technology game.

I love to eat and, true to my Southern upbringing, I am quite fond of barbecue in particular. Through my frequent visits to a barbecue restaurant in the area, I got to know some of the other customers, including a businessman who happened to develop websites in his spare time. We struck a deal, and he developed a business website for me, bringing Fitness3K into the digital commerce world. It didn't take long for the Fitness3K website to bear fruit. I received a phone call from a local high school baseball coach, inquiring about the use of the gym's batting cage for hitting lessons. It was a strong first step toward helping the marketplace understand what Fitness3K was all about, to realize the full scope of resources the gym had to offer. The coach, Jack Kuzniczi, toured our facility and it was the beginning of a prosperous relationship. Jack was a local legend of sorts, a coach with a long history of success who was well connected in the community. Jack gave hitting lessons in the batting cage and always seemed eager to introduce me to his clients, many of who also became clients of mine. It was a classy move by Jack and one for which I'll always be thankful. Little did I know that a few of those relationships were about to change my life.

One day, I walked into the batting cage area where Jack was working with a client. As usual, he was giving hitting lessons, but nothing else I witnessed was ordinary. The young batter to whom Jack was pitching was swinging the bat with one arm and connecting on most of the pitches. It was an amazing sight to see. The young man hit nearly all of the pitches Jack threw to him, and hit them hard. I was stunned. Jack saw my astonishment and introduced me to the young man. His name was Ryan Korengal. Ryan's parents, Don and Shelly, were also watching the session, and I had the honor of meeting them. What I'd seen Ryan do in the batting cage dominated my thinking the rest of the day. I wondered about his story, how and when he had lost the use of an arm and the impact it had on his life. All I knew was that Ryan had inspired me in a big way. As he made more visits to the batting cage to work with Jack, I began to learn of his story.

Ryan had been playing golf with friends one fall afternoon, when fierce winds blowing across the golf course from a Hurricane Ike–related storm front snapped off a large branch of a tree near Ryan, which fell on him and crushed his skull. He underwent life-threatening surgery to remove a large portion of his skull and part of his brain. His left side was partially paralyzed, and the injury had severely affected his mobility and impaired his eyesight. Given the challenging circumstances, surgeons at Children's Hospital in Cincinnati did an incredible job with helping Ryan to defy the odds stacked against him from such an accident. I've always believed that people cross our paths for God-given reasons, and I'm certain that was the case when Ryan crossed mine. Meeting Ryan was one of God's powerful ways of helping me to grow and to understand that there are so many people doing amazing things to overcome great odds, just as Ryan was doing despite incredible physical and emotional challenges. Witnessing Ryan's uncommon perseverance and determination made me want to be around him. I spoke with Jack about my desire to train with Ryan and help him in any way I could. I told Jack that Ryan had been a source of great inspiration to me and that I was compelled to offer Ryan any of my skills or knowledge as a trainer in return. Jack relayed my desire to Ryan's parents, who agreed to let me and Ryan work together.

My goal in working with Ryan was to help him improve his physical balance, which had been significantly affected by the trauma to his brain. I also hoped to help him build upper and lower body strength and to strengthen his core and begin to build his endurance. I aimed to complement the physical therapy Ryan was already receiving via Children's Hospital. I did my homework to learn about the particulars of that program so I could help Ryan build his strength in a way that was complementary. We began with functional exercises, which were focused on the movements he needed on a daily basis; these exercises were centered on his core. We worked with a medicine ball, which was a challenge for him given that he only had full use of his right arm and a very small percentage of his left. The fact that he had any strength at all in his arms was amazing to me considering that he'd been immobile in the hospital for a lengthy period after the accident. As Ryan and I trained together, his confidence grew in a big way and he made strong progress. He was able to perform exercises that showed his increasing upper and lower body and core strength.

The city's daily newspaper, *The Cincinnati Enquirer*, became aware of Ryan's story, including our training partnership, and came to the gym to interview Ryan and observe one of our training sessions. It brought me great joy to know that people were becoming aware of Ryan's story and were learning about what real strength and overcoming incredible odds truly mean and to know that he was inspiring others just as he was inspiring me. You might think that with all Ryan has been through since his accident, he would complain about the workouts once in a while or resist my pushing him hard to continue to challenge him in the gym. If he did, it would be understandable, but it's always been just the opposite with Ryan. The way he pushes himself to keep developing and getting better is amazing. In fact, Ryan has often pushed me to challenge him even more and continued to raise the bar on his own expectations for himself. His efforts and powerfully positive attitude have made me want to be better too. He has never seen his accident as an excuse to settle for a mediocre life. He believes in himself and what is possible and is pushing beyond the limits that constrain most of us so he can make a great life for himself and continue to inspire those around him.

Ryan Korengel

Ryan continued to push himself through high school and college. He went on to play golf and graduated from Mount St. Joseph University in Cincinnati, where he was awarded the David Toms Overcoming Adversity Award his sophomore year and is working to obtain an MBA. Witnessing his character and the work ethic and no-excuses approach Ryan displays on a daily basis has helped me to further understand what is possible when we refuse to accept limits on our lives. Ryan's father, Don, recorded video footage of Ryan's training sessions with me and shared the footage with Ryan's physical therapist at Children's Hospital. She was moved by what she saw of our synergy as teammates and how Ryan and I pushed each other in complementary ways during our sessions. After that, she began to refer potential clients to me. I felt honored and humbled, especially given my tremendous respect for the incredible work and first-class character the hospital and its team represent. When I think of my journey with Ryan and his impact on my life, my belief is reaffirmed that the people who come into our lives do so by God's design and that there are no happenstances.

I believe those moments and meetings are meant to be for all of us, including my opportunity to cross paths with Ryan and his family. Hopefully, we realize those moments and try to draw the best from them, to look for the life lessons there from God and to learn from those lessons to try to improve ourselves and help those around us. I believe Ryan came into my life at a time when I most needed it and he continues to help me grow and get better in ways he'll never know.

L-R: Jack Kuzniczi, Ryan Korengel,
Chideha Warner, Jim Reynolds

As I mentioned, each client with whom I have the opportunity to train is unique in terms of their goals and areas of desired development during our training sessions, and my duty is to design regimens for them that address those areas in the best way possible to help them. All my clients come with a unique set of life circumstances, and their stories continue to inspire me and make me work harder to keep improving, both as a trainer and in life outside of the gym.

I always try to understand the lessons in the stories clients share with me and to learn something from each of them that I can use to broaden my perspectives in life. My introduction to and experience working with a young man named Christopher Stock provided lessons beyond belief for me. I was introduced to Christopher by a longtime local baseball coach, Mike Stinson, a friend of the Stock family and a mentor to Christopher. At six feet, seven inches, Christopher's physical presence was impossible for me to miss when he walked into Fitness3K to meet with me. But contrary to his intimidating size, Christopher was soft spoken and shy, almost painfully so. Christopher's father was there too, and we began to discuss Christopher's background and training goals. At age four, Christopher had been diagnosed with Type 1 diabetes. Using an insulin pump, receiving shots, and closely monitoring his blood glucose levels had been a part of his daily life ever since. Christopher had played sports, particularly baseball, since he was a kid. He loved the competition, displayed great ability, and enjoyed the camaraderie that comes with being part of a team. Christopher was named the top player on the junior varsity baseball team as a sophomore at Moeller High School in Cincinnati. As a junior, he was among the top pitchers on the varsity squad, with a fastball clocked at nearly ninety miles per hour. He started the season 3–0 but was sidelined with a shoulder injury. He returned to action toward the end of the season and celebrated alongside his teammates as the club captured the 2015 state championship.

Christopher was regarded as one of the top baseball players in the area entering his senior year at Moeller and received interest from numerous colleges, including Ivy League member Brown University, which was a testament to his academic skill as well. His future appeared limitless. But then something changed for Christopher. The affable youngster turned reclusive, and he shied away from social situations and the interaction with friends he had previously enjoyed. His emotional slump continued to worsen and began affecting every part of his life. Playing sports, especially baseball, which had always been a source of great joy for him, began to feel forced and caused him great anxiety. When the time arrived for baseball team tryouts, he considered skipping them and was anguished throughout the process. When the season started, his motivation to practice each day and get better waned. Before games, Christopher would become agitated. He would suffer extreme stomachaches, often resulting in vomiting episodes. His performance in the classroom also began to suffer. Always an outstanding student, he became easily distracted and unable to study for tests or focus on even the simplest homework assignments. He also found it difficult to sleep.

At first, doctors believed Christopher's troubles were the result of anxiety and ADD. His parents attributed the anxiety to Christopher's uncertainty over his impending choice of college and major, but his problems grew more severe. He began to experience paranoia, including "hearing voices" in his head. Further evaluation of Christopher at the Lindner Center confirmed that he was suffering from schizophrenia and he underwent intense treatment. From February of his senior year in high school until summer break began, he missed all but one day of classes. Christopher's treatment caused extreme lethargy. He lost interest in going outside, preferring to stay in the house each day. Where he had previously thrived by getting to the gym and working out nearly every day, he chose not to go to the gym at all. His lack of exercise led to considerable weight gain. During the next several months, the medication he took provided a bit of relief, but he remained uncomfortable being outside the house or around other people. When he visited a gym near his house in an attempt to work out, he found the blur of noise and people overwhelming. Among those with who Christopher remained in contact during his ordeal was his former baseball coach, Mike Stinson. Mike happened to be giving hitting lessons in the batting cage at Fitness3K, and he shared Christopher's powerful story with me and asked whether I might do some personal training work with Christopher. I was moved by the opportunity of helping Christopher heal in any way I could.

Mike introduced me to Christopher and it was the beginning of a special relationship for me. I believe effective communication plays a key role in building and maintaining successful relationships with clients, and I try hard to establish a comfort zone with clients so they feel free to share their feedback with me about their training experience.

Feedback, good or bad, allows me to continue to grow and get better from a professional perspective. While I obviously hope that my clients always have a strong positive experience when working with me, I understand the reality is that may not always be the case. Whenever issues arise or clients wish to share some thoughts I may not love to hear, I want them to feel welcome to do so, without fear of hurting my feelings or believing it may make me upset.

Actually, as with anything in life, we tend to often grow more through times of adversity than during times when everything is going great, so I see strong value in all feedback, not just the positive stuff. I take it seriously and try to learn from my clients where I came up short and why and use it as an opportunity to get better. We all make mistakes, and it's what we do when we make them that matters. If we pay attention to what went wrong and learn from those experiences and adjust our game plan so that we don't repeat our mistakes, we'll keep improving. But if we become easily offended by honest feedback, especially if it's something about our approach or performance we may not necessarily wish to hear, then we're blowing valuable opportunities to grow and improve. In my training work with Christopher at Fitness3K, it seems the friendly, open atmosphere I work hard to promote has proved to be a comfortable fit for him. He indicated that it has allowed him to let his mental guard down and relax a bit so he doesn't have to feel overwhelmed or out of place. He has been free to focus his energy on his training, and it has paid dividends for him emotionally and physically.

As with my other clients, I have strived to create for Christopher a training atmosphere that includes a personal touch. In his case, having learned of his affinity for classic rock music that includes playing songs in the gym from legendary rock bands, such as Led Zeppelin and Pink Floyd. That music puts Christopher in his personal comfort zone so he can focus on and get the most out of his workouts. Again, it's about tuning in to and getting to know our clients so we know their likes and dislikes or triumphs and challenges in life. If they are just a number to us, just a dollar sign walking through our door, if as trainers we're only concerned about taking their money and sending them on their way, we're doing a big disservice to them and ourselves. That runs contrary to the nature of personal training, which should be about truly understanding others and their goals and helping them to reach those goals and more and to improve their physical and emotional strength, which can be life changing for any of us. It should be about providing that personal touch for them during the process. Christopher has made incredible strides toward recapturing his emotional and physical strength during our sessions and displayed a strong "no-excuses" approach to his work. He gives maximum effort each time and doesn't hold back, despite the ever-present challenge posed by his medication. He has progressed from resisting working out to being excited about coming to the gym. He has shown a rare courage and strength, and his efforts to overcome his challenges have inspired me. Despite the many obstacles Christopher has overcome and those he still faces, he has so much ahead of him in life, so much promise and possibility. I believe he'll accomplish anything he pursues.

Christopher Stock

He recently returned to baseball and the pitcher's mound for the first time in a few years, and the experience summed up Christopher's amazing character. He was invited to tryouts for a collegiate-level Champions League team in Cincinnati consisting of many talented prospects. He was understandably quite nervous when his turn came to pitch, and he even felt his body shaking. He walked to the mound, took a deep breath, and focused only on the catcher's glove. He pitched a full inning, and struck out two batters. Watching Christopher overcome his deepest fears and anxiety to pitch again and succeed was an incredibly emotional experience for his father. In a sense, Christopher had come full circle in his fight to bounce back from the mental anguish he had endured.

When I was developing my business plan for Fitness3K, I knew I needed to include a service to my clients that would help set me apart from my competitors in the marketplace. As a youngster, I became fond of boxing, a fondness no doubt aided by watching Mike Tyson destroy his opponents. I admired how he had risen beyond the poverty-stricken and dangerous environment in which he had grown up to become the youngest heavyweight champion in history. As a youngster, I was fascinated with boxing and thought I might pursue a career as a boxer. Thankfully, my parents dissuaded me, based on the significant head trauma involved in such a profession. Despite that, I love boxing and wanted to stay connected to the sport, which is why I became a certified boxing trainer. It has afforded me an opportunity to work with many professional boxers. Boxing has existed for centuries, and though there is no denying its brutality, there is a depth to the sport that many may not realize. It requires incredible discipline, tenacity and toughness, and strategy in the ring is vital to success. In many ways, those facets of boxing also apply to life in general. To succeed on a consistent basis and be at our best in the battles we continually face, we must be disciplined, tenacious and resilient, and we must have a plan. That's why I chose to add boxing to the training options for my clients at the gym. At the time, ours was the first gym in the Loveland area to offer boxing as a training option. Clients embraced it because it was therapeutic; it allows them to pour out their daily stress from work or home in a fun way through their punches. Boxing is a terrific multi-muscle group workout, and it builds self-confidence (especially for kids), burns a whole lot of calories, and helps improve balance and hand–eye coordination. Boxing workouts are known to have produced strong positive results with people suffering from Parkinson's disease and other ailments. I believe that there is much common ground between boxing and searching for the personal trainer who best fits your needs. After all, in both cases, you must do your homework. Boxers must know the tendencies of their opponent before they step into the ring, and it's the same with finding a personal trainer. We have to take the time necessary to find out about our prospective trainer, about his or her experience level and knowledge and commitment to us. In boxing and working with the right trainer, we must stay disciplined and accountable. The right mindset is crucial to success in both cases.

The Gym Timer is another distinct facet of the foundation of Fitness3K. Again, I created it as part of my mission to separate our gym from the competition. It allows for clients to stay engaged in their workouts and make maximum usage of their sessions, even if I am unable to be side by side with them during each repetition or exercise. I usually set the Gym Timer to one-minute intervals, with fifteen-second rest periods between. Instead of being forced to count each exercise rep, it allows us the freedom to talk or joke and learn about each other in the process. Depending on the particular exercise, it's equivalent to performing about fifteen-to-twenty repetitions. I'm always selective about using it, subject to a client's exercise performance ability, because, as we know, each of us has our own ability level, especially when new to the workout game. The Gym Timer helps clients keep themselves accountable and continue to push themselves during workouts as well as being a source of positive energy for them and me.

Besides training with clients in a one-on-one setting, I've been fortunate to work with a large spectrum of athletes. My experiences in working with teams began through an email I received from Christy Finch, an assistant lacrosse coach at the University of Cincinnati. Christy expressed interest in a personal-training relationship, and we designed a program for her that included boxing. Christy was pleased with the progress she made during our sessions and told her fellow lacrosse team coaches about it. The coaching staff came to the gym, which was the first step in what developed into a special relationship. From that meeting, I received an offer from the coaching staff to begin training the team. I was very comfortable with the personal training approach, but training with a team was a different and exciting opportunity for me. The team consisted of thirty-six members. I began by implementing a variety of sports-specific training stations for the team sessions, with a focus on essential core strengthening, which would prove to be immediately valuable to the team members in terms of additional on-field strength and endurance during games. In the off-season, the team had weekly training sessions with me at Fitness3K and several members of the team also did personal training sessions.

The team coaches were a huge help to me during the training sessions because they challenged the team members to push themselves beyond their previously accepted comfort zones and reach for their best, physically and mentally. The lacrosse team was a recent addition to the University of Cincinnati (UC) athletic program, and the coaches and team were making steady progress in workouts and in their approach to success. Unfortunately, the harsh reality of big-school sports is that success is measured almost exclusively by wins and losses, and because the team was not winning fast enough or as frequently as athletic department decision-makers might have preferred, the team's head coach came under scrutiny. I'm thankful for the opportunity I received from the UC lacrosse coaching staff to train them and the team's players. Training the coaches allowed me to develop friendships with them that continue to this day.

L-R: Lauren Schwarzmann, Christy Finch, Chideha Warner

Christy Finch and Lauren Schwarzmann received opportunities to again compete for spots on the US National Women's Lacrosse team (both had made the team last time around), and they sought my services to help them train in preparation. Each of them worked as hard as possible during training to be at their best for the tryouts, and I was honored to train with them. Lauren made the team again, but unfortunately, Christy didn't. She showed her strength of character by admitting that perhaps she hadn't been as focused and disciplined in her off-season diet and workouts the second time around, and she knew that it had likely cost her a place on the team. That honesty and accountability is a mark of great character. Christy refused to look for excuses for why she didn't make the team. Instead of looking to blame someone else for her situation, she was honest about where she had come up short and why, and that's the only way any of us in that situation can continue to grow and get better. If we're looking to find excuses or blame someone else for our situation, we're wasting valuable time and energy, because, ultimately, when we point the finger of blame at someone else, three fingers on that hand are pointing back at us. It always comes back to us. I believe that if we can't be honest with ourselves about our situation and what is necessary to improve in life, we'll remain stuck and fail to realize our potential.

The strong character Christy displayed contributed to her receiving an opportunity to become an assistant coach at Ohio State. Christy had a goal of becoming a head coach someday, and the opportunity at Ohio State was a valuable first step in that direction. I maintained my working relationship with the coaching staff at UC, which included training players and coaches new to the program, and continued to develop new friendships and connections. As a result, I received valuable opportunities to train with several select teams. Given the friendships I had developed with them, it was bittersweet to me when I received the news that Lauren was leaving her post at UC for a better opportunity at San Diego State and UC head coach, Lellie Swords, was stepping down and moving to Texas. It was tough because I drew inspiration from being around them regularly and would miss that connection with them, but I was very happy that they were doing what they felt was best for them.

Lauren Schwarzmann, Chideha Warner

As Fitness3K moves into its second decade, I'm thankful that I have been able to implement training programs for and work with a wide spectrum of athletes and sports teams. I fell in love with watching and playing sports as a youngster, and that fondness has only increased over the years. I love the between-the-lines competition aspect of sports but also have great respect and appreciation for the preparation necessary for top-level athletes to be at their best when they compete. They cannot hope to just show up and succeed without being physically and mentally prepared. We've all seen examples of teams or athletes who had great physical talent and showed up for a game expecting to win but lost because they had not prepared themselves in the best way possible; they had cheated themselves from a preparation perspective, and it cost them. I've enjoyed helping to guide and train athletes to be at their best on all fronts as they prepare for competition. That way, even if they lose the game, they can take some solace in knowing they gave their all in preparation, knowing they did not cheat themselves from a preparation perspective. But sometimes, even when we prepare in the best way possible, the other team is just better that day, and knowing that we adequately prepared makes it easier to live with that result. I take great pride in doing whatever possible for my clients to help them be at their physical and mental best so they can, each day, enter the battle of life well prepared. Each client has different needs, comes from a different perspective, and I respect that and try to tailor their workouts and training programs to those needs. From a life perspective, no matter our profession or position in life, I believe it's so important for each of us to try to help others succeed, because when they win, we win.

Recently, I received an opportunity to work with the Indian Hill High School girls' lacrosse team. The school's head coach asked whether I would help the team improve their speed and agility training during the off-season. I was happy to help, including working with the up-and-coming middle school players who would soon become members of the varsity team. Working with the Indian Hill program was very rewarding to me for multiple reasons.

First, as with all my clients, it was rewarding to watch each girl strengthen her work ethic and push beyond her established comfort zone to reach new levels of training performance. As the girls reached these increased performance levels, their desire to keep digging deeper to maximize their progress was fed; the improved personal training performance of each girl made her more accountable to her teammates, which raised the training performance bar for the team as a whole. As we know, when all team members are focused on the same goal and pulling in the same direction, special things can happen, and happen they did. They started the season strong and focused, and they never looked back. They won all but one game en route to capturing the 2017 state championship, the first ever for Indian Hill. The hard work they put in while training in the off-season paid off in a big way for them. They had made the commitment to take their training performance to a new level in preparation for the season and reaped the championship rewards as a result. They left it all in the gym and all on the field in pursuit of excellence and will always have a championship to show for their efforts.

Indian Hill High School Girls Lacrosse State Champions 2017

3K Movement Action Item

One thing I've learned is that you have to trust your instincts in every situation. I've made plenty of mistakes along the way, and I'm still learning and trying to find ways to enhance my craft in the personal training world. I think being one of the first boxing trainers in my area helped separate me from the pack. It's been a good trial for me to have clients who deal with enormous challenges, such as mental health, stress, or certain ailments. Boxing has been a huge outlet for them, and it is gratifying to me to know they enjoy the whole process of the positive relationship between the client and the trainer. Jim Rohn once said, "*Discipline is the bridge between goals and accomplishments.*"

Are your challenges feeling heavy? Take a moment to think about the challenges or even a defeat you've had in your life. How did you overcome the circumstance? Who have you crossed paths with who had an impact on you or inspired you? Tune into the 3K Movement podcasts, or send your questions in via the website Fitness3K.com. Remember, today's challenges are tomorrow's victories. Who knows? You may be the next guest speaker on our podcast!

Chapter 4

WHAT DEFINES SUCCESS?

To believe in yourself and to follow your dreams, to have goals in life, a drive to succeed and surround yourself with the things and people that make you happy...this is success!

Chideha Warner's daily affirmation

I try to begin each day by looking in the mirror and taking a few minutes to envision success, to plant that seed in my mind and heart before I head for work. Part of that process for me includes reaffirming daily a belief in my abilities, dreams and goals. I believe it is crucial for us to constantly reinforce for ourselves the things that truly matter to us in life so that we can focus our energies toward making those things happen and create a better life for ourselves and those around us.

Speaking of those around us, it's crucial that we surround ourselves with people who maintain good energy, believe in the tremendous possibilities this life offers, and are willing to commit to doing the work necessary to make those possibilities become reality. There's nothing worse than being surrounded by pessimistic or critical people who constantly drain our emotional energy and are always taking from others. These people often like to paint themselves as "victims," as people who just can't seem to catch a break. The reality is, though, that they refuse to give the effort necessary to improve their situation in life. Instead, they'd rather blame others for their mess and claim it's someone else's fault that they are stuck in neutral or reverse. They are in self-denial about the decisions that have created their circumstances and are more than happy to point fingers at everybody else. Their lack of willingness to look in the mirror and accept accountability for their choices keeps them stuck in life while they watch others who maintain positive attitudes and are doing the work continue to pass them by. We all know the difference between those who truly need our help and those just looking for a handout. We must avoid these self-proclaimed victims who are constantly seeking handouts but who refuse to commit to self-improvement or risk enduring the energy drain they bring. Surrounding ourselves with positive-energy people is a crucial factor in our realizing the success we're working so hard to achieve. After all, even a so-called normal day requires great effort and focus to overcome the challenges life throws at us, so maintaining a positive, can-do attitude and belief in ourselves is essential. If we're regularly allowing these negative excuse-makers to sap our valuable energy, we're costing ourselves our best opportunities to succeed. We are all essentially athletes in the game of life, and just as in sports, preparation is key to our success each day. We cannot afford to leave the house in the morning ill prepared to perform or with a suspect attitude.

Our thoughts set the tone for our actions, and we must maintain and regularly reaffirm for ourselves positivity and confidence and the belief that special things are about to happen for us. We attract what we think about; where our mind goes, our energy flows. If we're thinking positive things, it will show in our actions, and those actions will generate good results. We owe our family, friends and co-workers a good attitude, which is a strong example from which they can draw inspiration. No one wants to be around a bad-attitude energy-drainer.

Workouts are all about energy, and that energy extends far beyond the gym walls, before a client ever touches a piece of gym equipment. The energy reaches to the mental and emotional places that affect a client's mindset and work ethic when he or she gets to the gym. It's an ongoing process, which often gets lost in the bustle of our day-to-day lives. It seems we're always on the move, and if we're not aware or careful, we can fall into the dangerous trap of expending valuable energy where it's not truly necessary and then wonder later why we feel exhausted even before we get to the gym. We feel like we've already been through an intense workout that has left us drained.

That process of keeping good energy bottled up is vital to staying refreshed. If we think about it, there are numerous times during a given day when we're prone to letting our energy leak in the form of physical or verbal outbursts or needless comments or letting our minds race with fear or anxiety about some bad thing that might happen but likely will never happen. In truth, we work ourselves into a negative energy mindset about things that don't matter and never did, about things we insist on trying to control but have no way of controlling. It's all in our minds, and as we know, our minds affect our bodies in an undeniably powerful way. No matter what's happening around us, there are always two things we can control: our effort and our attitude. There's a whole lot of life that we can't control, including the actions, thoughts, or behavior of others. But we can always control our own work ethic (effort) and perspective about things or others (attitude). The world is a noisy place, and it seems everything is coming at us at warp speed. The constant barrage of information and technology and the endless onslaught of opinion and advice (much of it negative) at every turn can often leave us feeling overwhelmed. But when we strip it all away, we realize that no matter what someone else is saying or what is happening around us, we alone possess the power to control our effort and attitude. If we keep our focus during the day on maintaining good thought and behavior energy, on not letting our minds, mouths or behavior run wild, we allow ourselves to build a reservoir of emotional and physical strength that will guide our workouts when we get to the gym. We'll reap the benefits of being able to direct that additional powerful energy to our workouts, which will help us in a big way.

My duty to my clients when they arrive at the gym for their workouts is to tap into and help guide that energy source to ensure that they are making the most efficient use of their time and efforts to reach their desired results. It's perhaps the biggest key to the process of helping them reach their physical and emotional best because the two are intertwined. It's all about energy. It's about making continued progress. There is no room for just going through the motions with my clients. The way I see it, they are either moving ahead or falling back, and I refuse to let them fall back on my watch. That extends to their energy management beyond the gym, and to those aforementioned places that can either help or hinder them in their search for training success. Our physical and emotional exertion outside the gym can be costly and, if we're not careful in how we manage or fail to manage it, it can be downright dangerous to our health.

A case that comes to mind is Dave Kneuven, vice president of operations at Deerfield Construction. As a business executive with a hectic schedule, he faced daily stress levels that began to take a significant toll on his well-being. In 2001, Dave began experiencing abnormal and significant changes to his body. His legs quivered constantly and he lost his sense of physical equilibrium, making it difficult for him to stand without feeling dizzy. His speech became slurred. Doctors soon diagnosed Dave with Parkinson's disease and he eventually underwent deep brain stimulation, a neurosurgical procedure to reduce pain and tremors.

One day, Dave came into the gym to speak with me about working out to improve his physical conditioning. Dave began to work out and has never looked back. Our workout program, which includes boxing, is ongoing and remains focused on building Dave's core strength to improve his balance issues and hand–eye coordination. Despite his battle with Parkinson's, Dave's tenacity and no-excuses approach to his workouts are impressive, and he continues to inspire me.

It seems that whenever Fitness3K is open, Dave is there and working out. While participating in a local health fair,

I connected with Teresa Robinson, an outstanding personal trainer who focuses on working with clients who suffer from Parkinson's. I shared Dave's story with her and she offered invaluable insight on the management of Dave's workouts, which we have incorporated. Dave has made incredible progress through the years, including a tremendous increase in self-confidence and a belief that no matter what he faces in life, he will find a way to overcome it and thrive.

As far as success (and the generally accepted definition of it in our society) is concerned, I believe we often miss the mark. It seems most of us have become accustomed to viewing success through only a financial prism, equating success to varying levels of income. If a person makes an income we deem "sizable," for example, we see them as being more successful than someone who earns a lesser income. It's as if we assume that more money equals greater success and that success guarantees happiness, but that notion of success is an illusion.

Frankly, what is success anyway?

The reality is that success in life means something different to each of us. It depends on what's important from our individual perspective in terms of what we see as our true purpose in life. When I consider my own life thus far, money is far from the defining factor for me. I think about what I've accomplished in terms of making the most of the opportunity to open my own business, and I feel proud of what our team has been able to accomplish.

Fitness3K has been in business for over ten years, and I'm humbled to have been able to work with more than a thousand clients so far to help them improve their lives in some way. I think about all the pounds and inches these clients have lost on their way to better lives, and all the muscles toned and endurance and stamina built. When I think about these clients and the impact our relationships have had on my life and the progress we've made together, it reinforces for me the understanding that no matter what level of success any of us enjoys, we know it's never about us; none of us can do it by ourselves. If we're honest, we know there are many others who helped us (and continue to help us) along the way. Hopefully, we look for ways to help others succeed, just like those who helped us. That way, everybody wins. That's the true definition of success to me. If we're concerned only about what's in it for us, I believe we're missing the best that life has to offer. And, none of us can reach our goals without facing adversity along the way. That's just the way it goes. In the earliest days of Fitness3K, my operating budget was next to nothing and I endured a lawsuit that nearly crushed my dreams of doing business before I even got started. Also, shortly after opening the Fitness3K doors, the brutal economic recession of 2008 arrived, bringing with it a whole new level of pain and uncertainty.

The recession struck a blow across the US business landscape and it took no prisoners. New to the business ownership game, I had created a business plan about which

I felt confident in terms of addressing short- and long-term needs and potential obstacles and with an eye on steady growth. What I didn't foresee was the major negative impact the recession would have on my clients, many of whom were business owners themselves. Their businesses suffered significant slowdowns, which affected profits and caused serious concern about where those businesses and the economy might be headed in the longer term. It seemed that business as we had known it had changed overnight, and the reality was alarming to consider. The recession's impact caused me to rethink my business plan and to understand the importance of including a plan for when things go wrong, but in a positive way; not expecting them to go wrong, of course, but having a worst-case scenario plan in case there's a recession or some other unavoidable imposing factor. I personally saw the powerful effect of the recession on my business neighbor, Deerfield Construction, and it was eye-opening for me. Many of Deerfield's employees trained with me at Fitness3K and the stress of those times was apparent on their faces and in our conversations. The worst part for them and for all of us was that nobody had any idea how long the recession might last.

Deerfield's owners, Steve and Scott Bitzer, were forced to lay off numerous workers. There was plenty of pain going around, from companies, such as Deerfield, suffering financial losses to their employees losing jobs that provided for the well-being of their families to the families themselves wondering how bad things might get. Like many companies, Deerfield stayed the course, adjusting where necessary but refusing to yield to panic. Unlike many companies, they made it through the darkness of that recession thanks to the sound leadership of Scott and Steve Bitzer, who learned valuable lessons about making key adjustments from their father, Joe. Eventually, the market began to turn around, and Deerfield returned to doing strong business. The actions and cool-headedness under pressure exhibited by the Bitzers influenced me in a big way. Accordingly, I adjusted my own business plan, including the setting aside of and regular contribution to an "economic storm" fund. It was part of the growth I experienced during adversity. None of us wishes to face hard times, but making it through them provides us with lessons that can help us be better prepared when challenges arise again.

As we know, opening a business is one thing, but growing that business into a successful entity over an extended period of time is something else entirely. The Small Business Association states that 30% of new businesses fail during the first two years of being open, 50% during the first five years and 66% during the first 10 years in operation. That is especially true in the personal training industry. There are many factors that contribute to the high rate of business failure. A faulty business plan is ultimately a death strike, of course, but I also believe that many business owners in the personal training industry lose sight of why they got into the industry in the first place: to help others improve their lives. Granted, any business that doesn't make more money than it spends won't be around for long, so a profitable balance sheet is crucial to a sustained business operation. However, showing genuine care and concern for our customers—and being willing to go above and beyond for them—should always be front and center for business owners in this industry. After all, they are the lifeblood of our business; without them, we cannot succeed. If we're not focused on our clients and how we can serve them in the best way possible, based on their expressed desire and commitment to improve, we're in it for the wrong reasons.

We owe it to our clients to give them our best. If we take our customers for granted, we can bet they'll be gone. But if we're committed to giving them our best and working with them to dig deeply and pull the best out of themselves, knowing that their improved physical conditioning will have a powerful positive impact on their emotional conditioning and their lives in general, then we're in in for the right reasons. The development of those special relationships is what makes the whole thing work. That's the best possible payoff for our clients and for us. Giving of ourselves by looking for the best way to be of service to others is what we should strive to do. Like the legendary boxing champion Muhammad Ali said, "Service to others is the rent you pay for your room here on Earth." To me, our strong service to others to help empower them and improve their lives is the true definition of success.

My certification from the International Sports and Science Association, continuing education, and good fortune to cross the paths of the real movers in the personal training industry so I could learn from them and share that knowledge with my clients to help improve their lives in any way possible are invaluable currency. Learning from my clients and being inspired by their stories makes me want to keep getting better, and there's no price that can be put on that for me. As mentioned, surrounding ourselves with positive-energy people who are committed to finding ways to improve their lives and the lives of others is vital to our success. It's not always the "biggest moves" that make the most impact on us. The real magic is often in the more low-key moments, those meaningful moments of support or encouragement we receive from others. We can never take those moments of shared spirit or those who believe in us for granted. We must cherish the people and the relationships because life can turn quickly.

As a trainer, couples that are all-in with their workout regimen, who regularly come to the gym together on a mission to maximize their individual and partnership development, always impress me. These are couples that hold themselves and each other accountable, inside and outside the gym (including diet discipline), and they don't make excuses. They show up for their scheduled workouts without fail and continue that momentum when they leave the gym.

Mike and Donna Donahue were such a couple. They ran a successful business together and were a great complement to each other in terms of keeping each other in check on all fronts. They were very health conscious, especially Donna, who rarely allowed any bad food in her daily diet; she kept Mike in check when he was tempted to succumb to unhealthier dietary choices. In the gym, they became regular workout partners with fellow couple, Dave and Janet Zender. The couples worked out at the same time on Saturdays for more than a decade, sharing stories and perspectives and needling and pushing each other to keep improving. Where Donna and Mike were concerned, she was their driving, energetic force, and Mike acknowledged and embraced it. In the gym, for example, she was able to do more push-ups and sit-ups and jump higher than Mike, but she was always quick to encourage his efforts.

During one of those Saturday workouts, however, I noticed something unusual. Donna didn't seem to have her typical spark. She appeared fatigued early in her workout, struggling to catch her breath during exercises through which she typically breezed and requiring much longer breaks between exercises. As the weeks and workouts went on, Donna's situation worsened. Her skin began to turn yellow, indicating jaundice. It was alarming to witness the rapid changes taking place with Donna. She sought medical attention and underwent a battery of tests. The results were distressing: Donna was suffering from advanced colon cancer, which had spread to her liver. The survival rate for colon cancer at that stage is extremely low. Donna immediately began chemotherapy treatments and soon became too weak to train. Her illness led to the breakup of the couples' workout that Donna and Mike had enjoyed for so long on Saturdays with Dave and Janet.

Donna Donahue

Doctors told Donna the cancer had spread so aggressively and quickly that they didn't expected her to be alive for her next chemotherapy session, but she was a fighter and proved them wrong. She endured over fifty hours of chemotherapy treatment every other week, considerably more than a typical cancer patient receives. Donna continued to fight, but her illness worsened. She then began to receive in-home hospice care. Through our training sessions over the years, Donna and I had developed a special bond, and shortly before her death, she asked to see me a final time. She told me to take care of Mike and to keep pushing him to continue his workouts, and we expressed our love and appreciation for each other. Donna was one of the strongest people I have ever known, and she made an unforgettable positive impression on my life and business. She was a shining example of the value of the special relationships I have been blessed to develop with my clients, and I'm very thankful for it.

I believe we cross paths with people by God's design, that it's never just a random thing, and often those who cross our paths teach us in ways that change our lives. That was the case with a young woman named Claire Boyd, who signed up for a boxing class with me. Claire had been battling depression and the boxing workouts became great emotional therapy for her. Despite her depression, Claire showed great positivity toward me. She was always quick with a motivational quote and seemed to look for a way to share positive energy. Claire was a talented artist and she occasionally brought in drawings that expressed her moods to share with me. I respected Claire's spirit and the battle she was fighting and became one of her biggest fans during the time we trained together. Sadly, the emotional demons Claire fought ultimately became too much for her and she took her own life. I learned that I had been the last person to whom she had sent a text message the day she died. Her death was devastating to me. I fell into a depression afterward, just finding it so difficult to understand the loss of such a special young lady. I recently reached out to Claire's parents, Hank and Mary Ann, to let them know Claire will always hold a place in my heart and daily thoughts. We met for lunch and helped each other sort through some tough emotions. They understood the special relationship Claire and I shared, so they invited me to visit the church where Claire's ashes remain. Claire's spirit will always represent a strong beacon of light for me. Like Claire, many suffer from the fierce grip of deep

Claire Boyd

depression and battle to overcome it, seemingly rising beyond it at times to find happiness, only to lose all signs of hope and succumb to its devastating effects, including suicide. Sometimes, however, battling and overcoming depression yields a different result—a lasting message of hope from which others may draw inspiration.

Such was the case with a man named Mike Howard. His daughters, Kerry and Liz, who trained with me, introduced me to him. Mike and his wife, Kathy, had been married for over forty years. They were truly happy together, loved life, and seemed to have it all. Then their lives changed forever. In 2013, Kathy was diagnosed with ALS, Lou Gehrig's disease. She put up a valiant fight against her illness, but died in 2016. When Kathy died, Mike struggled mightily. He found himself steadily slipping into a dark emotional place from which he couldn't seem to escape. He had lost his best friend and soul mate, and he couldn't face life without her. His life seemed void of meaning and purpose. Mike's downward spiral eventually reached life-threatening levels. Night after night, he sat in darkness with a loaded pistol on his lap, contemplating suicide but unable to pull the trigger. His daughters had tried their best to support, console, and encourage him, and to help him understand how much they loved him and that life was worth living. Despite his strong initial resistance to their pleas, Mike eventually agreed to pursue some form of physical fitness, which brought him to Fitness3K.

Mike began to work out and, little by little, his spirit and demeanor changed. He had come to the gym a broken man, in deep sadness and with no seeming purpose, but with each workout, he began to see the light of possibility. Mike never stopped working out and improving his mental and physical conditioning, and he has become a powerhouse, a source of great strength and an inspiration to others. More important, he has become a friend. We have shared our life experiences the ups and downs of our journeys, including the darkness and pain he endured following his wife's death. He told me how our training sessions have changed his life, how they have pulled him from deep depression and given him renewed hope. He believes the workouts saved his life. I am thankful to Mike for his willingness to share his story and to use his own experiences in an attempt to help others who may suffer from depression, letting them know that no matter how dark it may sometimes seem, there is positive light ahead. His efforts to try to help others are what life is all about.

It's amazing to me the strength that is powerfully on display by so many around us who may be battling serious emotional or physical illnesses (or both) and how their strength in the face of those challenges can inspire us and teach us life's most important lessons if we're willing to pay attention and open our minds.

In that light, a man named Jack Wellman came to train with me, but when he came to the gym for his workouts, he didn't arrive in a typical fashion. Jack was afflicted with PSP (progressive supranuclear palsy), which affected the frontal lobe of his brain and caused significant problems with his balance, speech and eye movements. Because of the disease, Jack was unable to drive a car, but he didn't let that stop him. He was determined to get to the gym and train, so his wife or daughter drove him to Fitness3K twice a week. When he arrived, we'd help Jack from the car and into the gym.

Despite his severely limited ability to move his body, Jack wasn't the least bit discouraged or intimidated. In fact, he was intent on pushing himself beyond the limitations others set for him. He'd start his training sessions on the recumbent bike, for example, with a resistance level we set for him, but when no one was looking, Jack would quickly increase it to push his limits. His determination to get stronger was due in part to his desire to work with his children and grandchildren. A tough thirty-minute cardio session on the bike might have proved to be more than enough for someone else in Jack's condition, but not for him. He'd finish on the bike and continue to push for more training. He was especially interested in boxing training and loved working the heavy bag. The boxing work afforded Jack an opportunity to release his frustration with his illness by expending pent-up negative energy he felt because of it and reenergize his mind and body.

Because of his illness, Jack had great difficulty speaking, but his actions and energy spoke volumes for his strength and character. His commitment to get better despite the

Jack Wellman with his daughter Kathy

challenges he faced spoke to me in a big inspirational way. Because my relationship with Jack applies to the definition of "success," I feel blessed to have witnessed Jack's efforts and to have helped him get stronger. To me, that relationship and those sessions equal success. There is no dollar value that can define the strength I witnessed from him or the inspiration he provided me. Sadly, Jack died in 2011, but the lessons I learned from him about courage and the will to keep fighting will stay with me always.

I have been fortunate thus far to cross paths and train with several people who have inspired me with their work ethic and powerful positive attitude in the face of their own daunting health challenges, whether physical or emotional or both. These are people who, no matter the obstacles or odds they faced, have displayed their unique brands of courage and strength in the face of great adversity. While none of us would wish for others to face illness or disease, the fact is that I have witnessed amazing people showing what true character and strength is all about, people who have refused to allow themselves to be held hostage by their health challenges or physical conditioning and have committed themselves to working hard to improve their lives.

Though each of their stories is unique, these people are all great fighters who do not give up or give in to their afflictions or illnesses. They have refused to set limits for themselves, based on speculation from others, and have taken their situations into their own hands. As we know, the easiest thing to do when we're in the midst of great challenge is to give up; so to see them continue to push harder and refuse to accept built-in excuses is an incredible thing. Watching people like them battle to overcome great challenges brings to mind one of my favorite quotes from Dr. Martin Luther King, Jr., "The ultimate measure of a man is not where he stands in moments of comfort and convenience, but where he stands at times of challenge and controversy."

Hopefully, all of us learn from our life experiences, especially when we deal with adversity, as enduring those challenges makes us stronger and strengthens our character. I have faced my share of adversity along the way and learned valuable lessons from those difficult moments. No matter who we are, how successful we are, where we live, or how much money we make, one thing is for sure: each of us will face our share of struggles. That's the way it's supposed to be. Obviously, none of us wants to endure constant difficulty, but I don't believe life is supposed to be easy for us. After all, if everything we wanted in life were just handed to us and we didn't have to work hard for what we want or to make our dreams come true, there would be no emotional growth for us. We'd be emotional robots, void of all the valuable personal perspectives that make each of us unique and enable us to help others, thanks to the challenges we have faced. While there have been struggles in my life that have tested my emotional toughness and endurance in big ways and made me wonder if I were strong enough to get through them, I wouldn't change any of it. I believe each challenge teaches us something we need to know at the time. Hopefully, we pay attention and understand the lesson and use the experience to keep becoming a better person.

In life and business, solid planning is essential to putting ourselves in the best possible position for success. Yet, no matter how well we plan or what results we may anticipate, we also know that plenty of what we learn is from good old-fashioned trial and error, from having no previous experience at something but taking our best shot at it and learning by simply going through it. During my first couple of years as a business owner, I worked to stay active in the community so I could make connections and develop relationships with fellow business owners and others in the community to build awareness of Fitness3K in the marketplace.

Part of that marketing strategy included participating in local Fourth of July parades. With help from friends and clients, I distributed free Fitness3K promotional items in Loveland, including T-shirts and pens; we even gave away boxing gloves. I borrowed a big, bright-red Chevy Suburban truck to stand out among the parade crowd. The rear door of the truck opened to a large television and surround-sound stereo system blaring one of my training videos. I spent a big chunk of money for all these promotional gimmicks and assumed I would receive a big payoff with numerous new clients. The man who owned the promotional company with whom I was working suggested that perhaps I was overdoing things a bit as the owner of a business still in its infancy. Unfortunately, I didn't listen. I was too caught up in my anticipation of a big marketing win. I figured there was no way my investment in the promo items wouldn't pay

Chideha Warner, Parade Day 2009

off. I told my business associate, Pamela, to prepare for an onslaught of additional business that would blast Fitness3K into the business-growth stratosphere. I assumed (and we all know what can happen when we assume things) that my marketing work at the parades was all we needed to drive immediate and strong business growth. My assumption was incorrect.

During the two-plus-hour parade, we covered a large territory and distributed a small mountain's worth of Fitness3K business cards among the crowd. As I began the walk back to my car after the parade, I noticed a few of those business cards on the ground. As I continued to walk, I saw more and more of them on the ground. And more. And more. I was in disbelief at first and then I started to feel dispirited. It seemed that every card we had passed out was now laying in the grass, on a sidewalk, or along the gutter in the street. *How could this be happening?* I thought. *Didn't these people understand that part of my plan was that they were to hang on to those cards so they could begin calling us upon returning home?*

Nevertheless, I arrived at Fitness3K early the next morning in anticipation of an onslaught of phone calls and inquiries about Fitness3K membership from parade-goers. The morning passed without even so much as a call, as did the afternoon—no calls or stop-ins from potential customers. *It's Sunday*, I told myself. *They're all busy with church and family gatherings; they'll call tomorrow.*

Tomorrow will be a big day. But on Monday, the phones were deafeningly silent. Tuesday? Nothing. Wednesday? More of the same. The week went by without so much as an inquiry of any kind. I was baffled. After all, I had gone all out in my promotional efforts for the parade and spent lots of dollars on the flashy big pickup with the surround sound, given away free novelty items and covered the parade crowd with business cards. Surely, my efforts were not in vain. But still nothing. It was a painful learning experience for me, considering the dollars and effort I had spent to create a buzz. I adjusted my game plan for the Fourth of July parades the following year, including an additional parade in suburban Indian Hill, an affluent community near our Fitness3K location. Again, however, my efforts failed to generate additional business.

> *"What is defeat? Nothing but education; nothing but the first step to something better"*
> **–Bruce Lee**

Though I would obviously have preferred to see different results, those experiences helped me realize that tried-and-true word-of-mouth advertising is most effective for me. Nothing else before or since those days has worked better. I had learned that building awareness of Fitness3K and adding quality clients began and ended with providing superior service to my existing clients who would inevitably spread the word to friends, family members and co-workers. The same goes for my relationship with Fitness 3K vendors.

A key part of putting ourselves in a position to keep improving is choosing to let go of grudges and hostility toward others, instead of bottling them up. Keeping grudges alive causes us great emotional and physical harm and does nothing to help resolve the differences we have with others. When I was in the midst of my legal troubles with my former boss and the trainers whom I had hired upon opening Fitness3K, my first response was frustration and extreme anger. I couldn't comprehend why he seemed to want to cause trouble for me, and I quickly became bitter about the situation and those involved. It didn't do me any good to hold a grudge. But frankly, I allowed that bitterness to take root and it played havoc with my thoughts and emotions. It took me a long time to sort out those emotions and understand that I was only hurting myself.

> *"Holding hatred and revenge for someone is like swallowing poison and hoping it kills your enemy."*
> **–Nelson Mandela**

Isn't that the irony of it all? I can look back at that situation now and see the futility of my anger and resentment. I wish those trainers and my former boss the best. Despite having been fired and then sued by him, I eventually understood that through him, there were important life lessons for me to learn. For me, a key part of continuing to improve means a consistently strong focus on the needs of my clients and a constant consideration of how I can adjust their training sessions to best meet those needs. My customers are at the core of my Fitness3K mission statement, and I do not take that fact lightly. I am very grateful for the good fortune to work with each of them, and I realize that they are the reason I am able to do what I love for a living. Without them, my business would cease to exist.

I read my Fitness3K mission statement daily to continually reinforce my understanding of what this business is all about, which is serving others. That service is not about some convenient cookie cutter approach to their needs. Each of my clients is unique and has different training needs and goals in mind. They put their trust in me to help create the best road map possible for them to achieve those goals, and it's important that I deliver for them. That road map and drive to their individual progress and success includes shared accountability, inside and outside the gym. For example, from my perspective, it's not enough for me to simply guide them through a strong training session at the gym; I believe in keeping a line of communication open that extends outside the gym. That line of communication often includes discussion about their key life choices away from our training sessions, especially diet. If they're killing it during their workouts in the gym but eating poorly outside of it, they're costing themselves valuable progress toward their goals. They're holding themselves back, and I believe it's my responsibility to them to be truthful about the cost of those bad choices as it relates to achieving the training success they seek.

Providing quality service to our customers includes finding an important balance between maintaining professionalism and establishing a strong rapport with them. As a trainer working closely with my clients, I believe that developing that rapport means getting to know each client on a personal level in terms of what makes them tick—what motivates them and moves them to take action to improve their quality of life, physically and emotionally. Where do they come from? What challenges have they faced in the past or are they facing now? What are their goals for the training relationship? Where do they wish to go, and are they committed to doing the work necessary to get there?

Each of us is unique, and our individual journey in life is intensely personal. From a training and wellness perspective, taking a one-size-fits-all approach to working with our clients is an unacceptable, the easy way out. It's unfair to them. The only way we can design and implement a training program that works best for them is to develop that rapport, to get to know them as people so that we understand their self-professed strengths or areas of needed development. If we're not tuned in to each client's unique story or don't even care to take the time to learn it, we're missing the boat.

It's a "lifestyle" business, and that business extends beyond the gym or a particular training session. If we're truly tuned in to what we see and what they're telling us, we'll have a much better shot at designing regimens that are realistic for them, which helps to reduce any discouragement over the longer term. Witnessing the physical and emotional transformation of our customers is incredibly gratifying, and that transformation doesn't take place just by snapping our fingers. The commitments they make and work they do and the work we do with them along the way create their own kind of magic, a reward that can last a lifetime.

It's ironic to me that my passion is for personal training because establishing a business has been a huge training ground for me in terms of understanding the necessary fundamentals, the adjustments that must be made along the way and the commitment required to make it all work. Attempting to build and maintain a successful business over the long term requires the same intense focus and execution as a personal training regimen does. Just as in personal training, there is no shortcut to attaining that success. The desire and discipline to do things the right way each day are vital to achieving the results we seek. Although I wear the ownership hat at Fitness3K, I still believe my most important role is as a trainer. Why? Because my interaction with customers, that crucial customer-service side, is what hopefully keeps them coming back.

My role as a trainer constantly reflects the core foundational principles of my business, and those principles are on display for customers to see. In each situation with my customers, it's my duty to make them feel important, to establish an atmosphere of trust and comfort for them, and to help them understand that I'm committed to doing whatever I can to help them reach for, achieve, and maintain their fitness and lifestyle goals. Each of my customers is valuable to me, and I'm thankful for the opportunity to work with them. I strive to never take them for granted because competition is fierce. I understand that if they don't believe I am tuned in to what they're telling me and they feel in some way that they are just a number to me and that I'm not truly invested in helping them succeed, they may be gone quickly, never to return. And that's a surefire way to business failure.

Ultimately, the message of my mission in life is that we're all here to help each other and to find ways to use the skills with which we've been blessed to make things better for those around us. Because like it or not, we're all teammates in this game of life, no matter our race, gender, sexual orientation, or political views or whether we're tall or short, fat or thin, or anything else. We're here to improve society, not to sabotage others' dreams or cause them problems. If we're looking for ways to get better and to make our teammates better, the whole team wins. If we're just in it for ourselves and focused on only what we can get from others instead of seeking ways to give, we're part of the problem.

The mentors, such as my grandfather, who have helped to set a positive tone for my life have been about finding solutions, not just complaining about problems, and that starts with striving to be our individual best, physically and emotionally. If we're cheating ourselves or taking shortcuts in our individual growth and improvement, there's no way we can help others reach for their best. We all know this world can be a crazy place and there are constant challenges to overcome, but I believe that when we work together, great things are possible.

No matter the industry in which we work, networking is key to establishing and driving success. There are people out there who want to help us, and it's up to us to make the effort to find them. Big or small, no potential business connection is insignificant. We must work our connections each day to keep ourselves ahead of the game and our competitors, especially early on. More than half of all new businesses fail within the first four years of operation, so it's important for us to pinpoint our business niche and seek to clearly define what separates us from our competitors.

The foundation of Fitness3K is to help others reach for and become the best possible version of themselves. As we know, being at our best physically creates powerful, positive emotional energy; the two work hand in hand. It's an amazing cycle as each continues to feed the other. And that individual energy can't help but have a positive influence on those around us.

3K Movement Action Item

Even though I've made a difference in numerous peoples lives as a trainer, I still feel like I was put on this earth to do more, which means networking with people who can help me reach others or help people I'm currently working with. Bill Nye once said, *"Everyone you will ever meet knows something you don't."* That's why I enjoy going to networking events; networking is sometimes better then currency because you don't know where that next handshake may take you. What's your favorite part of networking? Who have you made a difference for, or who has made a difference to you? What do you think you have been put on this earth to do? What more do you think you can do to make a difference? What success stories can you share with The 3K Movement?

ABOUT THE AUTHOR

 Chideha Warner is a longtime personal fitness trainer, business owner, life coach, and believer in the power of purpose and using our knowledge and skills to help others to achieve success, inside and outside the gym. Warner owns Fitness3K in Cincinnati and is considered by industry experts among the top fitness and sports performance trainers in Ohio. Warner is certified by the International Sports Sciences Association (ISSA), USA Boxing, and Boxing Fitness Institute and is a member of the National Strength and Conditioning Association (NSCA),

the worldwide authority on strength and conditioning. Warner specializes in personal, group, and corporate fitness training and in college and youth fitness agility and sports performance programs, along with training a large spectrum of athletes. Warner's unique training approach is rooted in the tailoring of effective programs to clients' specific needs—a relationship-based focus rather than the common personal fitness training industry approach of one size fits all—thus ensuring his clients the best opportunity to achieve lasting training success.

Warner was born in Bryan, Texas and reared in Atlanta before his family moved to Baton Rouge, Louisiana, where Warner resided from intermediate school to high school at University Laboratory High School—LSU. Warner went on to graduate with a BFA from Grambling State University before relocating to Loveland, Ohio, a suburb of Cincinnati, where he resides today.

Printed in the USA
CPSIA information can be obtained
at www.ICGtesting.com
JSHW080001150824
68134JS00021B/2201